Fermen... ow
to Fern ...es

by ... Johnson

Disclaimer:

This information is provided for consumer informational and educational purposes only and may not reflect the most current information available. This book is sold with the understanding the author and/or publisher is not giving medical advice, nor should the information contained in this book replace medical advice, nor is it intended to diagnose or treat any disease, illness or other medical condition. Always consult your medical practitioner before making any dietary changes or treating or attempting to treat any medical condition.

This information does not cover all possible uses, precautions, interactions or adverse effects of the topics covered in this book. Do not disregard, avoid, or delay seeking medical advice because of something you may have read in this book. Always consult your doctor before adding herbs to your diet or applying them using any of the methods described herein.

While we endeavor to keep the information up to date and correct, we make no representations or warranties of any kind, express or implied, about the completeness, accuracy, reliability, suitability or availability with respect to the book or the information, products, services, or related graphics contained book for any purpose. Any reliance you place on such information is therefore strictly at your own risk.

It's important that you use good judgment when it comes to fermented food. Do not consume food you think may have gone bad bad because it looks, smells or tastes bad. The author claims no responsibility for any liability, loss or damage caused as a result of use of the information found in this book.

Dedication:

This book is dedicated to all those who have discovered the many benefits of fermented food. I'd like to thank my friends and family, who were kind enough to taste test the recipes for this book. Thanks guys! I couldn't have done it without you.

Contents

What is Fermentation?

Fermentation is one of the oldest food preservation techniques known to man. The process of fermenting foods is efficient and inexpensive, and it requires little by way of scientific knowledge or special equipment. Fermentation is the only food preservation technique that makes food healthier instead of damaging.

The *fermentation process* is a natural chemical process in which yeast or bacteria convert carbohydrates into lactic acid or alcohol in an anaerobic or near-anaerobic environment. When done properly, fermenting food encourages the growth of healthy microorganisms, while seeking to prevent the growth of microorganisms that cause food to spoil or go bad.

In addition to preserving food, fermenting breaks some of the substances food is made of down into simple components the body is able to recognize and quickly process into energy and nutrients. Fermented food is full of living organisms that are beneficial to the human body. This stands in stark contrast to most of the foods consumed today, which are largely devoid of healthy organisms.

There are a number of food items created using the fermentation process. Here are just some of the foods made through fermentation:

- **Beer.**
- **Fermented fish.**
- **Kefir.**
- **Kimchi.**

- **Pepperoni.**
- **Pickles and other pickled vegetables (if the proper pickling process is used).**
- **Sauerkraut.**
- **Some breads.**
- **Some cheeses.**
- **Wine.**
- **Yogurt.**

Yeast is used to convert sugar into alcohol during the brewing process for beer and wine. While the alcoholic brewing process is an interesting process, it isn't covered in this book.

What is covered is the *lacto-fermentation process*, which is the process used to ferment vegetables. Special bacteria known as *lactobacillus* are used in the lacto-fermentation process. Lactobacillus bacteria are able to create lactic acid out of the natural sugars and starch found in foods. Lactic acid prevents food from going bad by preventing the growth of harmful bacteria. In addition to warding off harmful bacteria in food, lactic acid plays an important role after it's been consumed by promoting the growth of healthy bacteria in the digestive system and making the food it's found in healthier and easier for the body to digest.

Fermentation Preserves Food

Fruits, vegetables, milk and other food items are perishable and have a very limited shelf life when left unpreserved. Take the same foods and ferment them and you've created foods capable of lasting a lot longer before they go bad.

Fermentation slows the rapid deterioration raw foods are prone to after they're harvested. When foods are left untreated, they quickly deteriorate to the point where they're no longer edible. This process can be slowed by refrigerating the food items, or it can be drastically slowed down by food preservation techniques like canning, freezing, drying and fermenting.

Failure to properly preserve sensitive foods opens them up to attack from harmful microorganisms. We've already talked about the healthy bacteria formed by fermenting. There are also bad bacteria that can form in food as it ages. These unhealthy bacteria break down the food, leaving waste products behind that taste bad and can cause serious health problems in those who consume it. The toxins in spoiled foods run the gamut from harmless toxins that change the texture and flavor of the food as it spoils to downright dangerous toxins that can make you very sick or even kill you.

The fermentation process creates an environment in which unhealthy bacteria have trouble taking hold and growing. Bad bacteria need oxygen to thrive and fermentation takes place in a largely anaerobic environment. This environment encourages the growth of healthy bacteria, which only need tiny amounts of oxygen to grow. By depriving vegetables of oxygen by submerging them in brine, the fermentation process promotes the growth of probiotic bacteria, which are the good bacteria the body needs to thrive.

Fermenting food extends shelf life exponentially. A food that would normally go bad in a matter of days can last months or sometimes even years after fermentation. Placing fermented foods in the refrigerator after allowing them to ferment unchecked for a while at room temperature further extends shelf life because it slows fermentation to a crawl.

Being able to ferment foods gives you the ability to save food items long after they would normally have gone bad. Large amounts of produce can be grown and harvested and then fermented or otherwise preserved and saved for harsh winter months when food might be scarce. The ability to ferment foods also allows you to take advantage of great deals on produce when it's in season. You can buy more food than you'd normally be able to consume before it went bad and ferment what you aren't able to use immediately.

Another benefit of learning how to ferment food is it gives you the ability to preserve food in a manner that doesn't require electricity. We largely rely on our refrigerators and freezers to keep our food fresh. What, then, would happen if an emergency situation took place that left us without electricity for an extended period of time? With fermentation, we'd be able to preserve much of our food before it went bad.

Sure, we could can some of it and dry some of it, but the fermentation process is one of the more forgiving food preservation techniques. Learning to ferment food not only helps you live a healthier life now . . . It could help you help yourself in an emergency situation.

Why It's Better to Ferment Your Own Food

Spend enough time around people who ferment food and you'll undoubtedly hear someone say fermentation is more of an art form than it is a science. The lacto-fermentation process doesn't lend itself well to large-batch fermentation because it's tough to produce consistent results. Even when fermentation methods are standardized, the end product won't consistently be exactly the same every time—which is what consumers expect from off-the-shelf products.

For this reason, most manufacturers use brining methods that mimic fermentation in flavor and texture, but don't feature the same healthy bacteria you get when lactobacillus is used. These manufacturers use techniques that slow or completely eliminate the formation of healthy bacteria in the name of more consistent results. Most people don't know or don't care about the health benefits of proper fermentation, so it's a win-win situation for the manufacturers. They sell a lot of product and they don't have to worry about the problems associated with lacto-fermentation.

In addition to slowing or stopping the enzymatic process, there are often a number of chemicals and preservatives added to pickled vegetables sold in stores. Instead of getting a healthy fermented food like you would if you fermented it at home, you're consuming a food that's been bathed in a chemical cocktail that's likely doing more harm than good.

When it comes to health value, products sold in stores are more often than not a shadow of what they'd be if you made them yourself at home. The best way to make sure you're getting the health benefits of properly fermented foods is to ferment them yourself. That way you have ultimate control over the fermenting process and what goes into your foods.

Fermenting vs. Pickling

You may recognize a lot of the recipes in this book as items you commonly see on supermarket shelves. Pickles, sauerkraut and relish are all common items sold in grocery stores and found in pantries and refrigerators everywhere. You can walk in pretty much any grocery store and find pickled items on the shelf. It would be easy to make the assumption that the items sold in supermarkets are made via the same fermentation process used when these items are made at home.

For most of the products sold in stores, that assumption would be incorrect. While there are a select few companies making true fermented foods, most manufacturers have taken the easy way out by using pickling methods that are easier to control, but don't have the same health benefits as truly fermented foods. Most manufacturers use vinegar for pickling and don't bother with fermentation. When vinegar is used for pickling, there are no live bacteria or enzymes left in the food.

In addition to using vinegar for pickling, manufacturers also use heat and pressure to cook the foods, further killing any probiotic value they may have had. They then add chemicals to prolong shelf life, which do nothing more than line the manufacturer's pockets. They've taken what should be healthy probiotic foods and turned them into food items that are easy to mass produce, but are a ghost of what they are when pickled and fermented at home.

It's important to realize that not all pickled foods are fermented.

Pickling, by definition, means preserving food in some sort of acidic brine. That brine can be a result of the fermenting process, which creates lactic acid that preserves the food, but it doesn't have to be. Pickling brine can also be made up of other acidic mediums like vinegar, which is the most commonly used brine in commercial products. When vinegar is used, fermentation does not take place and foods pickled with vinegar do not have the same healthy probiotic cultures fermented foods do.

When you ferment foods at home using the methods described in this book, you're creating living foods packed with healthy bacteria. The homemade vegetables you're making are still pickled, because they're preserved in lactic acid. In addition to being pickled, they're also fermented, which is an additional process that walks hand in hand with pickling. It's the fermentation process that allows healthy bacteria to stick around and grow. These bacteria then create lactic acid as a byproduct, which pickles the food while it ferments.

When you do find true fermented foods on store shelves, you'll end up paying a pretty penny. The manufacturing process is difficult to control, especially when large batches are made, so manufacturers charge more money for fermented foods. You can make the same probiotic foods at home for a lot less money and it really isn't hard to do once you've learned the ropes.

To sum the difference up, pickled foods are foods that are preserved in acidic brine. Fermented foods undergo a process in which healthy bacterial cultures are formed. Some pickled foods are fermented, but the ones typically sold on grocery store shelves aren't. The best (and cheapest) way to ensure your pickled foods are fermented and contain probiotic cultures is to ferment them yourself at home.

Fermenting Vegetables

Vegetables are one of the easiest foods to ferment, making them a good place for beginners to learn the ropes. Vegetables can be fermented using only the organisms found on the vegetables or starter cultures can be added to jump-start the process. The biggest difference between the two processes is the fermentation process takes longer when starter cultures aren't added to the mix.

There are two key components required for fermenting vegetables: *brine*, which is salty liquid, and vegetables. That's it. Anything else you add is above and beyond what's required.

There are two basic methods used to ferment vegetables. The *airtight-container method* uses a sealed container like a mason jar. The *airlock method* uses a container that's left "open" to off-gas during the fermenting process through use of an airlock lid designed to let gases out while keeping oxygen from getting in is placed on the container.

Here are the basic steps required for brining vegetables using the airtight -container method:

1. **Wash the vegetables and the container you're using.** Don't use too hot of water or anything that will kill the healthy bacteria found on the vegetables. The container should be clean, as well as any utensils that come in contact with the ingredients going into the fermenting container.

2. **Cut the vegetables up into pieces.** The smaller the pieces, the quicker the fermentation process will be. Some recipes call for vegetables to be left whole. This is fine, but will slow down fermentation.

3. **Add sea salt to the vegetables.** If the vegetables are fresh and moist, the sea salt will draw water from the vegetables, creating brine from the moisture contained within the vegetables. Shredded vegetables will release the most moisture. You can help the vegetables release moisture by squeezing them or bruising them a bit.

4. **Add water, if necessary.** Some vegetables will release enough water when you add salt that you won't need to add additional water. Other vegetables won't release enough water, especially when the vegetables are left whole, as is the case when fermenting larger items like cucumbers and carrots. When adding water to create brine, add 2 to 4 teaspoons of sea salt to each quart of water you have to add.

5. **If you're adding starter cultures, add them now.** Whey, kefir grains and a number of other starter cultures can be added to get the fermentation process off to a good start. This step isn't always necessary, but it will make things move along at a faster clip.

6. **Place the vegetables and brine in a glass jar.** Some people use a Crockpot for fermenting, but I prefer a jar I can seal. Besides, I use my

Crockpot way too often to have it tied up fermenting vegetables. Any glass jar with an airtight lid will do.

7. **Press the vegetables down into the jar to eliminate any air pockets.** This step is crucial because any air pockets left where air can come in contact with the vegetables are places where the vegetables can go bad. The vegetables need to be completely covered with brine and there should be no trapped air left between the vegetable pieces.

8. **Weight the vegetables down.** Place a weight in the container and press it down to hold the vegetables below the surface of the brine. Keeping the vegetables submerged is critical to preventing mold and keeping the fermentation environment anaerobic.

9. **Fill the jar to within an inch or two of the top with brine before sealing it.** Make sure you don't leave too much room for trapped air at the top of the jar. It's also important not to fill the jar all the way up because the fermentation process releases gas and the contents of the jar can expand. It's rare, but there's a chance of the jar exploding if too much gas is trapped in the jar.

10. **Put the lid on the jar and seal it tightly.**

11. **Store the jar at room temperature.** The jar should be sealed and left in a warm area for up to a couple days. If you're planning on fermenting the vegetables for more than a day or two, be

sure to open the jar periodically to release pressure. Tremendous amounts of pressure can build up in a sealed jar during the fermentation process and the only way for them to escape is to open the lid. If you do open the lid, make sure you reseal it properly and don't leave air trapped inside the jar.

This method of fermenting is used successfully by people across the globe. It's a viable fermenting method that has been shown to work effectively. That said, I don't really like this method. Here's why.

When you're fermenting foods, you want to keep oxygen away from your food because it will cause all sorts of problems, from the formation of mold to causing certain chemical compounds in both the food and brine to oxidize. Having to remove the lid to off-gas and check the food every day or two allows oxygen into the jar. While you may be able to get away with it, there is an increased likelihood that the food you're fermenting will go bad because of the oxygen you're allowing into the jar. Those using this method should make every effort to keep the vegetables being fermented submerged in brine.

The airlock method is similar to the airtight-container method, with a few key differences. Here are the steps required for the airlock method:

1. **Wash the vegetables and the container.** Don't use hot water or anything that will kill the healthy bacteria or inactivate the enzymes. The container and any utensils used to handle the contents of the container need to be clean.

2. **Cut the vegetables up.** Unless you're planning on pickling them whole, then move on to the next step.

3. **Add sea salt.** 1 to 3 tablespoons per quart should be sufficient.

4. **Squeeze or bruise the vegetables a bit with a solid object to get them to release juices.** This step is optional. Fresh vegetables with a lot of moisture will often release enough liquid that you won't have to add water. Gently mashing them can help them release more liquid.

5. **Add water, if necessary.** If you need to add water, now's the time to do it.

6. **Add the starter culture, if you plan on using it.** Now's the time to add your cultures. If you planning on letting your vegetables ferment naturally, move on to the next step.

7. **Place the vegetables and brine in a glass container.** You can use any glass container you want, as long as you can keep the vegetables submerged in it and there's an airlock lid available. Leave a few inches of empty space at the top of the container.

8. **Use something to press the vegetables down until they are completely submerged in the brine.** In order for the fermentation process to work correctly, the vegetables have to remain submerged in the brine while fermenting. They should not come in contact with open air.

9. **Place a weight on top of the vegetables to keep them submerged.** It doesn't matter what

you use as long as it is made of a material that won't react to the brine and is capable of holding the vegetables beneath the surface of the brine.

10. **Place an airlock lid on the container.** The airlock lid should be designed to let pressure and gas out, while keeping air away from the fermenting food inside. Manufacturers sell a number of airlock lids capable of being attached to all sorts of containers. Follow the instructions that came with the lid to properly seal it.

11. **Store the container at room temperature until it begins to ferment.** Keep the container in a warm area of your house until it has fermented to your liking. The ideal temperature for most fermented vegetables is 72 degrees F.

Special fermenting containers and crocks are sold in stores that are designed to keep air away from vegetables while allowing gases to escape. If you plan on fermenting regularly, it would be a good idea to invest in a couple of these containers. My personal favorite containers are the Pikl-It containers. A 1-liter container will cost you around $20. If you don't want to spend the money on new containers, you can buy airlock lids that will fit mason jars for less than half that price.

Containers of fermenting vegetables should be kept in an area where the temperature is as close to 72 degrees F as possible. This is the optimal temperature for vegetable fermentation. Fermenting in too cool of an area will slow the fermentation process to a crawl.

If you don't have a warm enough area in your house to place your containers in, you can place them under an incandescent bulb or two. Wrap the containers in towels and place the light over them. Make sure the light is far enough away that it doesn't warm the containers too much, but is close enough to warm them to the desired temperature.

The Health Benefits of Fermented Vegetables

One of the most common fermented food items are vegetables. There are a number of health benefits associated with fermenting vegetables. Here are some of the many ways fermenting vegetables can benefit the human body:

Fermented foods have more vitamins. Fermented foods have been shown to have elevated levels of folic acid, B vitamins and riboflavin, amongst other things.

They help with digestion. Fermented foods are partially digested. This helps your body finish breaking down foods it would normally have trouble with. The carbohydrates in the foods are partially broken down during the fermentation process, making it easier for the body to digest them. An example of this is the lactose found in milk products. Yogurt, kefir and cheeses that have been fermented are easier for the body to digest because the lactose is already partially processed before it's consumed.

They're probiotic. Fermented foods promote the growth of healthy bacteria in the digestive tract. We need healthy bacteria in our body. Properly fermented foods encourage the growth of the bacteria the body needs to properly digest the food we eat.

Probiotic foods help the body absorb more nutrients. A properly balanced digestive system creates an environment in which the body is able to process and absorb larger amounts of nutrients from food.

They give the immune system a boost. Fermented foods keep the digestive system running like a well-tuned machine. When the digestive system isn't healthy, the body has to dedicate resources to keeping the digestive system in good order. When the body is firing on all cylinders, the immune system is able to dedicate more resources to warding off infection and disease.

Studies show a number of diseases and health conditions can be helped by eating probiotic foods. There are a large number of studies covering more than 150 different diseases that can be helped by consuming foods containing healthy bacteria. From obesity to the common cold, fermented foods may be able to help.

Fermentation preserves food. The fermentation process creates an environment in which harmful bacteria are unable to grow. This allows for the preservation of food items with having to freeze them, can them or dry them. Learning to preserve food allows you to save food for a longer period of time without having to worry about it going bad. It also allows you to save food without damaging it.

Fermenting foods is an inexpensive and easy way to preserve your food while enhancing its health value. While most food preservation techniques damage food, fermentation makes it better by adding beneficial bacteria and nutrients. Combine fermented food with a natural or raw diet and you'll create an environment in which food is easy to digest and your body is able to glean as much as possible from every bite you take.

Buying Supplies: What You Need to Get Started

I thought about taking the easy way out and listing brine, vegetables and a container as the only things you need, but decided to flesh this chapter out a bit. While the previous three items are the only things you absolutely need, there are a number of other items you can have on hand that will make life easier.

Here are the items you're going to want on hand if you're serious about fermenting vegetables:

- **A knife and cutting board.** You're going to need something you can use to cut up the vegetables before you put them in the container. Alternatively, a food processor can be used to quickly process large amounts of food.
- **A container.** Canning jars can be used in a pinch. Ceramic crocks and airlock jars created specifically for fermenting are a better choice.
- **Weights.** A weighting system should be used to keep the vegetables below the surface of the brine. As they ferment, they're going to want to float to the top, where they're more likely to be exposed to air. Placing a weight on top of the vegetables will ensure they stay below the surface of the brine. A heavy piece of glass or a ceramic plate are good choices for weighting devices.
- **Unrefined sea salt.** Sea salt draws moisture from the vegetables. It also slows the fermenting

process a bit. Don't use iodized salt because it has iodine added, which can prevent beneficial bacteria from growing. You also want to avoid salt that has anti-caking agents added. Pickling salt, which is basically table salt with the iodine and other additive removed, can be used in place of sea salt.

- **Filtered water.** Filtered water is used to clean the vegetables and to create brine if the vegetables don't have enough moisture. Tap water with added chlorine and/or fluoride can be problematic when it comes to culturing vegetables because they can stop fermentation dead in its tracks.
- **Starter cultures.** Whey, freeze-dried cultures or kefir can be used as a starter culture. We cover starter cultures later in this chapter.
- **Vegetables.** This should go without saying, but you're going to need vegetables. Fresh vegetables work best, so don't wait until your vegetables are on the verge of going bad to ferment them.

Using a Fermenting Crock

Fermenting large amounts of vegetables in small containers can be an exercise in frustration. Instead of a single fermentation to watch, you have multiple containers you have to keep an eye on. This can be a real hassle if you're trying to make large amounts of fermented food.

A better option is to invest in a fermenting crock or two. Instead of having to deal with multiple smaller containers, you can fit more than a gallon of vegetables and liquid into the average crock. Some of the larger fermenting crocks hold up to 4 gallons and, if you really want to go all out, there are 50-liter crocks on the market. That's more than 13 gallons you can ferment at once!

Switching over to using crocks allows you to make larger batches of food with ease. Most fermenting crocks come with 2 stone or ceramic weights, each of which is a half circle. You put the ingredients and the brine in the crock and place the weights on top. The weights are then pressed down until they're below the surface of the brine. If there isn't enough brine, more brine can be added. The weights hold the vegetables underwater during the fermentation process.

Most crocks come with a trough onto which the lid to the crock is placed. This trough should be filled with water before placing the lid on the crock. The water creates an airlock that keeps outside air from entering the crock, creating an anaerobic environment in which fermenting can take place.

There is usually a notch cut into the lid. There has to be enough water in the trough to cover this notch. The notch is there to allow gases to escape from inside the pot as fermentation takes place. When the pressure gets high enough the gases inside the crock will push their way through the water and escape. Don't leave the notch exposed because this will allow oxygen into the crock.

Why Add Salt?

Salt fermentation is one of the oldest food preservation techniques known to man. Our distant ancestors found that food lasts longer when packed in salt and have been doing it in one form or another for thousands of years.

While salt isn't absolutely necessary for fermentation to take place, it helps the process by pulling moisture out of the vegetables and creating an environment in which the good lactobacillus bacteria can thrive. It prevents harmful bacteria from forming, and in the process gives beneficial bacteria a chance to grow unchecked.

It's important to realize salt slows the fermentation process down. The more salt you add, the slower the process will be. Be careful not to add too much salt, because it will cause fermentation to grind to a halt. Too much salt will kill both good and bad bacteria, rendering the food a dead zone in which no bacteria will grow.

Less salt equates to faster fermentation and a more biodiverse environment. The problem with using less salt is it tends to make the vegetables less crisp. If crisp, crunchy pickled vegetables are your goal, use a bit more salt. If you don't mind softer vegetables, less salt allows for more healthy bacteria to grow. When you use less salt, you might find there is a white film that develops at the top of your jar. This isn't a problem. This is yeast and it can be removed and discarded.

When adding salt to water to create brine, 1 to 3 tablespoons per quart of water is sufficient. If you add 3, you're going to have salty brine that ferments slowly. Most people find that vegetables fermented in this salty of a brine taste too salty. Any more than 3 tablespoons of salt per quart of brine and you run the risk of stopping the fermentation process.

Salt-Brining Techniques

Brining is the process in which salt water is added to vegetables to help create an anaerobic environment in which fermentation is able to safely take place. Self-brining fermentation occurs when only salt has to be added, while *water-added brining* occurs when water has to be added in addition to salt.

When salt is added to fresh vegetables, the salt pulls moisture from the vegetable itself. The finer the vegetables are cut or shredded, the more moisture the salt is able to draw out. When vegetables are able to create their own brine without water having to be added, the brining process is called self-brining. Self-brining works well with fresh vegetables like cabbage that naturally contain a lot of moisture.

Most vegetables that are self-brined are grated to ensure salt comes in contact with large areas of the surface of the vegetables. The salt draws moisture out of the vegetables at every location it comes in contact with it. Grated vegetables have more surface area than whole vegetables, so the salt is able to leach more water from them.

Self-brining doesn't work well when vegetables are left whole or cut into larger pieces. There isn't as much surface area for the salt to come in contact with, so less water is pulled from the vegetable. When using large pieces or whole vegetables, water-added brining is a better option. With water added brining, enough water is added to ensure the vegetables are covered in brine. The amount of water added depends on the size of container the vegetables are in, but a good rule of thumb is to leave at least an inch of water over the top of the vegetables.

When you add water, it will dilute any salt you've already added. 1 to 3 tablespoons of sea salt or pickling salt can be added for every quart of water you add. The more salt you add, the slower the fermentation process will go. Don't add too much or fermenting will grind to a halt.

Water-added brining is usually easier than self-brining because you don't have to chop vegetables up and wait for the salt to draw the water from the vegetables. If you're looking to save time while preparing foods for fermenting, you can really speed things up by adding brine and using larger pieces of vegetable.

Starter Cultures: Are They Really Necessary?

Recipes for fermented vegetables often call for use of some form of starter culture, which are cultures added to the recipe to get good bacterial growth started. These cultures are added to recipes in order to speed up the fermentation process and help ensure good bacteria take hold before the bad bacteria can start growing. Freeze-dried cultures, kefir grains and whey are all commonly used starter cultures you may see in recipes.

There's a lot of debate in the fermentation community as to whether starter cultures are a necessity. Traditionalists point out the fact that starter cultures are a relatively new phenomenon and have only been added to the fermentation process in recent years. Their basic premise is foods have been fermented for thousands of years without the use of starter cultures and people got along just fine. Why start using them now?

Starter cultures are bacterial cultures that give the fermentation process a helping hand. When you use a starter culture, you are inoculating the brine with healthy bacteria. Instead of relying on the naturally-occurring bacteria to grab hold and take over, you're speeding up the process by creating an environment that contains large amounts of healthy bacteria from the get-go.

There are a number of starter cultures in use today. Here are some of the most common:

- **Freeze-dried cultures.** These are live cultures that have been inactivated via freeze-drying. These cultures come with specific instructions that have to be followed to bring the cultures back to life.

- **Kefir.** Kefir can be added as a starter culture by mixing it into the brine when you add the vegetables. Kefir is available in grain form or as a powdered starter culture. The grains have more healthy bacteria strains in them, making them the more biodiverse option. When kefir grains are added to milk, they can be reused over and over again. When they're used to ferment vegetables, they're typically only used once.

- **Liquid from a previous fermentation.** Adding a couple tablespoons of brine from a previous fermentation to a new fermentation can help get the bacterial growth off to a healthy start.

- **Probiotic capsules.** Some people break open a probiotic capsule and drop the contents of the capsule in the brine to speed things up. Probiotic supplements contain large numbers of beneficial bacteria.

- **Whey.** As long as you can handle dairy, whey can be used to add healthy bacteria to a vegetable ferment. There are a number of processes through which you can make your own whey from dairy products that contain live cultures like buttermilk and some yogurts.

Starter cultures jump-start the fermentation process, but they aren't a critical addition for most vegetables. Fresh vegetables should have plenty of good bacteria already growing on them. It's up to you whether you add them. If you want to speed the process up, add some form of starter culture. On the other hand, if you want to ferment foods naturally, leave the starter cultures out. It's recommended that, at the very least, you add salt.

If you peel the vegetables you're fermenting, it's a good idea to add starter cultures because a lot of the beneficial bacteria will be tossed out with the peel.

When Is Fermenting Complete?

While most recipes will provide a range of days as a general guideline as to how long certain foods need to be fermented, it's largely a matter of choice. As fermentation occurs and more healthy bacteria form, vegetables take on a tart taste. The longer they're allowed to ferment, the sourer they're going to taste, but the more beneficial bacteria they'll have.

Remember earlier when I said fermenting is more an art than a science? This is where the art part comes into play. You're the artist and your fermented foods are the canvas. You decide how long to paint, or ferment, the foods. The longer you ferment them, the more healthy bacteria the foods are going to have, but they're going to have more of a tart kick to them. Some people love the extra tang, while others aren't able to tolerate it. This is the reason some people prefer fermenting their vegetables for only a few days, while others opt to ferment for a couple weeks or even months.

There are a lot of variables involved when it comes to timing fermentation.

If you use a lot of salt, fermentation will be slow. Too much salt and your food won't ferment at all. Containers stored in rooms that are warmer than 72 degrees F will ferment faster, while containers in cooler rooms will ferment slower. Even when conditions appear to be the same, fermentation may not occur at the same rate every single time. This is why commercially fermented foods aren't fermented inasmuch as they've been brined using vinegar and other methods that don't create the same probiotic environment as true fermentation.

Monitor your vegetables closely as they ferment. Some vegetables only need a couple days to ferment. Others need a couple weeks. For most vegetables, 1 to 2 weeks creates the best balance between flavor and healthy bacterial flora. Once the initial fermentation is complete, move your fermented vegetables to the refrigerator. This slows, but doesn't completely stop, the fermentation process.

The fermentation process is an easy one, but it's one that takes a bit of practice to get right. If you're able to perfectly ferment vegetables on the first try, pat yourself on the back. If not, learn from your mistakes and try again. Once you get it, it's like riding a bike. It gets easier and easier every time you do it.

Most fermentation recipes in use today call for a quick fermentation at room temperature followed by slow fermentation in the fridge. There are a handful of items to look for that indicate it's time to move the fermenting vegetables to the refrigerator:

- **The brine has started to bubble.** This is a natural reaction that takes places as lactic acid starts to form. These bubbles are gases created by the bacteria as they process carbohydrates in the vegetables. If you don't see bubbling, don't worry too much. The bubbling can be subtle and you may not see it easily. Fermenting foods only bubble for a while, so later stage fermented foods won't have the same amount of bubbles as foods that just started fermenting.

- **The fermented vegetables smell sour when you open the lid.** A sour smell is good. A rotten smell isn't. Good fermented foods can have a strong smell when the container is opened for the first time. Take a piece out and let it sit for a little before checking the smell. If it smells rotten, throw the vegetables out and start over again.
- **The vegetables have a fermented taste.** Properly fermented vegetables have a sharp, tangy flavor that's unmistakable once you've tasted it. Smaller vegetables will start to taste fermented before larger vegetables will.

To sum it up, look for bubbles and a sour smell first. When the first two items are noticed, it's time to taste the vegetables to see if they've fermented to your liking. If there are any indicators the food has gone bad, throw it out and start over again. Remember that a food that tastes strongly sour already is only going to get stronger over time, even while refrigerated. Whenever you check your vegetables, make sure all of the vegetables in the container are covered by brine before you put the weight in and the lid back on.

The only way to completely stop fermentation is to either freeze or boil the fermented food, which will kill all of the healthy bacteria. Even refrigerated foods slowly continue to ferment, like a fine wine. This is the reason why fermented vegetables left in the fridge for a couple months often taste better than they do when they were first put in the refrigerator.

To answer the question, fermenting is never 100% complete. There's somewhat of a fine balance between properly fermented vegetables and vegetables that have been allowed to turn into a soft mush, so watch your fermented foods closely.

Storing Fermented Vegetables

Storing fermented vegetables is easy. Once your vegetables have fermented to your liking, move them from the warm room to the fridge. This will slow the fermenting process down, ensuring your veggies last a long time. Alternatively, fermented vegetables can be stored in a cool root cellar.

Store the vegetables in an airtight container and make sure they stay submerged in the brine in which they were fermented. This allows them to continue fermenting. Removing them from the brine will expose them to oxygen, which will cause them to go bad and start to rot. The only time your vegetables should be exposed to air is when you take them out of the container to eat them.

Airlock containers are great for fermenting vegetables at room temperature. They aren't necessary when you move the vegetables to the fridge. Replace the airlock lids with regular airtight lids and screw them down tightly to ensure your fermented vegetables have a long shelf life.

Properly stored vegetables can last 6 to 8 months in the fridge or longer before they start to degrade. They won't last as long in a cool root cellar, but should still last at least a few months.

How to Tell If Fermented Vegetables Have Gone Bad

It isn't a common occurrence, but batches of vegetables do go bad from time to time. There are a number of signs to look for that may indicate fermented vegetables have gone bad.

The easiest way to tell if fermented vegetables have gone bad is to open the lid and inhale deeply. Good fermented vegetables will have a tangy, sharp odor to them. Vegetables that have gone bad will often have a rotten stench. Once you've learned what properly fermented vegetables smell like, you'll be able to easily tell when vegetables smell rotten.

In addition to a rotten stench, there are other items to look for that may indicate harmful bacteria are growing instead of beneficial bacteria:

Mold. There is some literature that indicates mold can be scooped away if it starts to form on the top of the vegetables. This may not be a safe practice. Mold sends out invisible tendrils that could be invading the food beneath it. While the vegetables beneath the moldy ones *might* be fine, the formation of mold is indicative of an aerobic environment in which bad bacteria are able to grow. I'm not willing to take a chance by eating food that's *probably* fine. If you see mold, it's best to throw out the batch of vegetables and start again.

NOTE: It's important to differentiate between mold and yeast. Sometimes greyish-white yeast will develop and float to the top of the water. This isn't mold and can be poured off.

Brown spots. A brown color is indicative of food that has come in contact with oxygen and is starting to rot.

The food turns to mush. While the fermenting process will eventually break food down until it goes soft and gets mushy, rotting food will turn to mush at a faster rate.

Slime. Food that's going bad can take on a slimy texture. If your vegetables feel slimy and soft, they may be going bad. Slime can also invade the brine, turning into a thick mucus-like substance. If this occurs, toss the vegetables out.

Rotten taste. It's important to note that your palate is your final line of defense when it comes to telling whether or not a food has gone bad. If food is displaying any of the other indicators, it shouldn't be tasted. That said, food that looks perfectly fine can sometimes taste a bit off when you put it in your mouth. If it doesn't taste right, don't eat it.

Lack of bubbles. Bacteria create gases as they process food. If there are no bubbles, this may be a sign there are no healthy bacteria present. Wait a day or two to see if bubbles start to form. If not, give it another day or two. If nothing has happened after a week, there's a pretty good chance fermentation isn't going to happen. It's important to remember some foods bubble a lot more than others and the bubbling can be rather subtle with certain foods.

Your senses are your best defense against foods that have gone bad. Never eat anything that doesn't look, smell or taste right. Eating food that has gone bad can make you extremely sick, so it's best to err on the side of caution.

Properly fermented vegetables are generally considered safe to consume. That said, there is the occasional batch that goes bad, either because too much oxygen was allowed in or there were other conditions that allowed harmful bacteria to take other. Remember, if something doesn't feel right, it probably isn't. If you aren't sure if your vegetables are good or not, throw them out and make a new batch.

How to Make Your Own Whey from Yogurt

Making fermented vegetables using the vegetable starter culture packets sold in stores can get a bit expensive. Good starter culture packets run anywhere from $2 to $4 per packet of cultures. The cost of starter packets can really start to add up for someone doing a lot of fermenting.

The good news is you don't have to use starter packets unless you want to. Wild fermenting doesn't use starter cultures at all, and is a good option if you have time to wait for the bacteria to grow on their own. Those looking to speed things up without spending a small fortune on starter culture can make their own whey from probiotic yogurt or buttermilk.

Here are the items you're going to need to make your own whey:

- **String.**
- **A glass bowl.**
- **A large piece of cheesecloth.**
- **2 cups of buttermilk or organic yogurt.**

Lay the cheesecloth flat on your counter and place the buttermilk or yogurt in the center of the cloth. Draw the four corners of the cheesecloth up and tie the corners together with the string. If done right, you will have created a cloth sack with the buttermilk or yogurt in it.

Find somewhere to hang the bag. If you have kitchen cabinets that hang over a counter, you can tie the bag off to one of the cabinet handles. It doesn't matter where you hang the bag, as long as it's room temperature and the bag is suspended in the air from the string tied to it.

Place the glass bowl beneath cheesecloth bag. The center of the bowl should be lined up with the center of the bag, so anything that drips from the bag lands in the bowl. The liquid that makes its way through the cheesecloth is whey. As long as you used probiotic yogurt or buttermilk, the resultant whey will be packed full of healthy cultures.

Leave the yogurt or buttermilk hanging for 3 to 4 days to allow the whey to separate from the curds. The whey collected in the bowl can be added to your cultured vegetables (and other fermented foods) to jump-start the fermenting process. The whey can also be added to smoothies and other foods to give them a probiotic boost. Most fermenting recipes call for approximately ¼ cup of whey.

One more thing—don't throw out the curds left inside the cheesecloth. They can be used the same way you'd use cream cheese. Add it to dip, spread it on a sandwich or eat it on crackers.

Lacto-Fermented Vegetables Recipes

The recipes in this chapter all use lacto-fermentation to create fermented vegetables. Vegetables rank amongst the easiest foods to ferment, so they're a great place to get started fermenting.

Don't limit yourself to the recipes in this chapter. Once you've learned to ferment these vegetables, you can pretty much ferment any vegetable you want. Don't be afraid to experiment. Some of my best recipes came from trying new things to see what they taste like. When attempting something new, make a small batch first, so you aren't stuck with a big batch of a fermented vegetable you don't like.

Simple Sauerkraut

This is the first recipe in the book because it's one of the most popular fermented foods around. The word sauerkraut directly translates to "sour cabbage." It's easy to make and cabbage contains large amounts of healthy bacteria, so you can get away with not using starter cultures (unless you want to).

When making sauerkraut, the cabbage used should be fresh and full of moisture. This will allow you to make sauerkraut using the self-brining method, with no water added. This first recipe uses only sea salt and cabbage to create basic sauerkraut.

Ingredients:

2 heads of cabbage

2 carrots

2 tablespoons unrefined sea salt

Directions:

Wash the cabbage and carrots. Chop the cabbage into small pieces or place it in a food processor. The type of cabbage you use is up to you. It really doesn't matter, as long as it is clean and fresh. Try combining a couple different colors of cabbage for an interesting look. Peel the carrots and grate them.

As you chop the cabbage, bruise it a bit by pressing on it with a blunt object like a kraut pounder and sprinkle a light dusting of sea salt onto it. As you add the salt, place the cabbage in the container you plan on fermenting it in. The salt will immediately begin to draw water out of the cabbage. A couple tablespoons of salt are all you'll need.

Pack the cabbage and grated carrot into the container as tightly as you can. Add a bit of cabbage, pack it in tightly and then add more. Continue the process until the container is full to within a few inches of the top. Once the container is full, place a weight that fits tightly into the container on top of the cabbage and press it down into the container. The weight should be heavy enough that it stays in place once you press it down. If it isn't heavy enough, place something heavy on top of the weight. The weight needs to be pressed down hard enough to ensure there are no air pockets left in the sauerkraut.

Cover the container for 12 hours. Uncover the container and press the weight down again. There should be enough moisture to where the weight is submerged beneath the surface of the brine. If not, you may have to make some brine of your own to add to the container. Add a tablespoon of sea salt to a quart of water and pour as much as you need into the container.

Seal the container and set it in a warm room to ferment. The perfect temperature for fermentation is 72 degrees F. Cooler temperatures will slow the fermentation process, while warmer temperatures will speed it up.

The sauerkraut will start to noticeably ferment after a couple days. How long you allow your sauerkraut to ferment before you move it to the fridge is up to you. Some people prefer the taste after a couple days of fermentation. Other prefer a couple weeks or even a month or longer. Leave your sauerkraut fermenting for too long and it'll become soft and mushy. Once your sauerkraut has fermented to where you want it, move it to the fridge.

Make sure you use sterile utensils to remove sauerkraut from the container as you eat it. Clean the weight and replace it, repacking the sauerkraut so the weight is once again below the surface of the brine.

When you start to get low on sauerkraut, you can make a new batch using the old brine that's left over after you use all the sauerkraut. The brine will contain large amounts of beneficial bacteria that'll get your new sauerkraut off to a good start.

Gourmet Sauerkraut

I love experimenting with sauerkraut to see what delicious recipes I can come up with. This gourmet sauerkraut recipe is a spin on the simple sauerkraut recipe, but instead of using normal cabbage, I seek out heirloom cabbage types that are a bit more exotic and grow them in my garden.

If gardening isn't your thing, heirloom cabbages can sometimes be found at farmers markets. You never know what you're going to find at a good farmers market and I've lucked out a few times and found interesting cabbages I was able to use to make sauerkraut. They weren't exactly cheap, but the sauerkraut was good enough to justify the extra cost.

I call this sauerkraut gourmet sauerkraut because it's a delicious and special treat that can't be had all the time. The caraway seeds and dill seeds add a bit of flavor to the sauerkraut and really add to the recipe. You can also add a tablespoon of juniper berries if you want even more flavor.

Ingredients:

2 heirloom cabbage heads

1 teaspoon caraway seeds

1 teaspoon dill seeds

1 teaspoon juniper berries (optional)

2 tablespoons unrefined sea salt

Directions:

Wash and core the cabbage heads. Chop them into fine pieces. As you chop them, add the sea salt to the cabbage and place it in a large bowl. Use a kraut hammer or another blunt object to press the cabbage into the sides of the bowl.

Add the caraway seeds, dill seeds (and juniper berries, if you decide to use them) to the bowl and stir them into the sauerkraut. Divide the contents of the bowl into the container(s) you're using. If you're using a crock, the entire bowl should fit into the crock.

Place a weight in each container and press the weight down, packing the sauerkraut into the container tightly. It should be tight enough so there are no air pockets in the sauerkraut. Cover the sauerkraut and let it sit overnight. Press it down again in the morning. The brine should be over the top of the weight. If not, make more brine by adding a tablespoon of sea salt to a quart of water and add brine to the container until the weight is covered.

Put the lid on the sauerkraut and let it sit at room temperature for a week. Check it after a week. If it has fermented to your liking, move it to the fridge. If not, let it sit for another week or two, checking it every couple days. Once the sauerkraut has fermented to the point where you think it's done, move it to the fridge or a root cellar.

Cucumber Sauerkraut

If you like pickles and sauerkraut, you're going to love this recipe. By adding cucumbers, onions and black pepper, you get sauerkraut that's crunchy and manages to be both sweet and spicy at the same time.

Ingredients:

1 head of cabbage

1 large cucumber

1 sweet onion

1 clove garlic

1 teaspoon cracked black pepper

1 dill sprig

1 teaspoon caraway seeds

Starter culture (optional)

2 teaspoons unrefined sea salt

Filtered water

Directions:

Wash the vegetables. Shred the head of cabbage. Add the sea salt to it as you shred it and place it in the fermenting container. Mash the mixture up a bit to help the salt pull the water out of the cabbage. Slice the cucumber into chunks. Cut up the onion and mince the clove of garlic. Add all of the vegetables to the container. Add the black pepper, dill sprig and caraway seeds and stir them into the mix.

Add the starter culture and stir it in. The starter culture is optional and isn't a necessity.

Dump the vegetables into the container(s). Place a weight in the container. Press it down as far as you can. There may not be enough liquid to push the weight below the surface of the brine. If not, put the lid on the container and wait overnight. Try again the next day. If you still can't press the weight below the surface of the brine, add brine to the container until you can.

Put the lid on the container and wait for 1 to 2 weeks. Check the sauerkraut regularly and move it to the fridge when it's fermented to your liking.

Cultured Coleslaw

Coleslaw is normally made with raw cabbage. It's good, but can cause problems with digestion, as raw cabbage can be a bit tough for the body to digest. Cultured cabbage is partially broken down, so it doesn't cause the same problems. You get all the benefits of coleslaw (and then some), without the flatulence and other digestive issues non-fermented slaw tends to cause.

This coleslaw is made using the simple sauerkraut at the beginning of the chapter. If you have another favorite sauerkraut recipe, you can use it. All that matters is the cabbage in the recipe has to be fermented.

Ingredients:

3 cups simple sauerkraut

½ cup mayonnaise

½ teaspoon celery salt

Salt and pepper, to taste

Raisins (optional)

Pineapple (optional)

Directions:

Whip up a batch of simple sauerkraut. This recipe requires planning in advance because it takes at least a couple days for the simple sauerkraut to ferment.

Take 3 cups of simple sauerkraut and place it in a glass bowl. Add the mayonnaise to the bowl. Season it with celery salt, salt and pepper, to taste. You can add the raisins at this point, if you want to add them. You can also add pineapple, if you'd like.

Stir it all together and serve cold.

Kale Slaw

You probably haven't heard of kale slaw. There aren't too many people who have. It uses kale instead of cabbage to create a fermented slaw that's tasty and has all the healthy benefits of kale. If you want this slaw to be more like regular coleslaw, try adding a dollop of mayonnaise to it and stirring it in before you eat it.

Ingredients:

3 cups kale leaves

2 carrots

1 cup small broccoli florets

½ medium onion

Starter culture (optional)

1 tablespoon unrefined sea salt

Filtered water

Directions:

Wash the vegetables. Chop or shred the kale leaves. Shred the carrots. Cut the broccoli florets into small pieces. Dice the onion. Place all of the vegetables in a glass bowl and mix them together.

Create brine by combining the sea salt with 4 cups of filtered water and stirring the salt in until it dissolves. Add the starter culture now if you're going to use it. Place the vegetables in the fermenting container. Pack them in tightly. Pour brine into the container until it's just over the top of the vegetables.

Place a weight in the container and press it down to squeeze any air pockets out of the vegetables. The brine should be over the top of the weight when you're done pressing it down. Make sure you leave a couple inches headspace at the top of the jar because the salt in the brine will pull more moisture out of the vegetables.

Place the lid on the container and let it ferment at room temperature for up to a week. Check it after a week and move it to the fridge if you're happy with the fermentation. If not, let it ferment until you feel it's ready.

Horseradish

Horseradish is one of those foods you either love or hate. It's hot, but the uncomfortable heat is what endears it to its many fans. Making horseradish at home requires exercising extreme caution, as the oils in the horseradish can burn your eyes and any other soft tissue they come in contact with. Horseradish is so hot and full of volatile oil, just being in the same room with a freshly cut chunk of horseradish can make your eyes water.

In case you were wondering, the chemical in horseradish that gives it such a potent kick is *allyl isothiocyanate*. This chemical forms when the cells of the horseradish are damaged. It's designed by nature to drive animals that bite into it away. Don't let it drive you away, as horseradish is antibacterial by nature and this horseradish recipe is a great probiotic condiment for meats and salads.

Ingredients:

2 cups fresh horseradish root

Starter culture

2 teaspoons unrefined sea salt

Filtered water

Directions:

Wash the horseradish root and peel it. Chop it into fine pieces or grate it. Place the horseradish in a blender and add the sea salt. Blend the horseradish into a paste.

Add the starter culture and a few tablespoons of water to the horseradish and blend it. Continue adding water and blending it in until the horseradish is the consistency you want it.

Transfer the contents of the blender to the fermenting container. Place the lid on the container and let it sit at room temperature for 5 to 7 days. Move the fermented horseradish to the fridge once it starts fermenting.

Good Health Ferment

I originally started making this recipe because I enjoy the taste. Then a funny thing happened. I noticed that colds and the flu didn't seem to last as long and I don't seem to get sick as often when I'm eating this recipe. Maybe it's because it's high in vitamin C . . . or maybe it's the cultures in the veggies. I'm not sure exactly why it works so well; it just does.

Ingredients:

1 head of cabbage

1 jicama

½ cup fresh spinach

1 cup small broccoli florets

½ medium onion

¼ cup fresh orange juice

1 teaspoon orange zest

Starter culture (optional)

1 tablespoon unrefined sea salt

Directions:

Clean all of the vegetables. Chop the cabbage, jicama, spinach, broccoli and onion into small pieces. Alternatively, add them to a food processor and chop them up.

Mix the vegetables together in a bowl. Add the sea salt to the bowl and stir it into the vegetables. Add the orange juice, orange zest to the bowl. Add the starter culture at this time, if you want to use it. Stir everything together.

Place the vegetables and juice in the container(s) you plan on using. Add a weight and press it down until the weight is beneath the surface of the brine. If there isn't enough brine, add water until the weight is beneath the surface of the brine.

Put the lid on the container and let it sit at room temperature for 5 to 7 days. Check it after 5 days to see if the vegetables have fermented to your liking. Once the vegetables have fermented to your liking, move the container to the fridge.

Simple Cultured Beets

I wasn't sure I was going to like this recipe. I've never been a big fan of beets, and until I tried this recipe, I'd never met a beet I enjoyed eating. This recipe changed my mind about beets. These beets taste great on their own and go well with most salads.

Ingredients:

10 beets

Starter culture (optional)

2 teaspoons sea salt

Filtered water

Directions:

Wash and peel the beets. Preheat your oven to 325 degrees F and roast the beets until they soften up. This will take between 2 and 3 hours, depending on how soft you want them. Roasting isn't absolutely necessary, but I've tried them both ways and think they're much better roasted.

Slice the beets into ¼- to ½-inch pieces. Place the beets into your fermenting container. Add filtered water until it's over the top of the beets. Add the sea salt and starter culture (if you're using it).

Place a weight on top of the beets to keep them below the surface of the brine as they ferment. Press the weight down and add water if necessary. The weight should be below the surface of the brine.

Seal the container and let the beets ferment for3 to 4 days before opening the container and checking them. Once the beets have fermented to where you want them, move them to the fridge.

Pickled Ginger Beets

This recipe is similar to the previous beet recipe, but it adds honey and ginger to the mix. The touch of honey combined with the ginger and spices give these beets a unique flavor that's tantalizingly delicious. Some people add a bit of orange juice or orange zest to this recipe to add even more flavor.

Ingredients:

10 beets

2 tablespoons raw organic honey

3 tablespoons shredded ginger

½ teaspoon cinnamon

1 teaspoon allspice

Starter culture (optional)

1 tablespoon unrefined sea salt

Filtered water

Directions:

Wash and peel the beets. Slice them into round pieces or chunks.

Add the honey, cinnamon, allspice, starter culture and sea salt to 3 cups of filtered water and stir it until the honey and salt have dissolved. Place the beets and the ginger in the fermenting container and pour the brine into the container until it covers the beets.

Place a weight in the container and press the weight down until it's submerged below the surface of the brine. If there isn't enough brine, add filtered water to the container until the weight is covered.

Place the lid on the container and let the container sit at room temperature to 5 to 7 days. Check the beets periodically and move them to the fridge once they've fermented to your liking.

Beet Sauerkraut

Beet sauerkraut consists of half beets and half cabbage. The red in the beets leaches out into the brine, creating a deep red sauerkraut that's both tasty and a sight to behold.

Ingredients:

1 head of cabbage

2 medium beets

1 clove garlic

1 teaspoon caraway seeds

Starter culture (optional)

2 tablespoons unrefined sea salt

Filtered water

Directions:

Wash the vegetables. Shred the head of cabbage and peel and shred the beets. Mince the garlic. Place the vegetables in a bowl and sprinkle sea salt over the top. Let them sit for 5 minutes and pound them with a sauerkraut pounder. Alternatively, you can mash the vegetables with your hands. Add the caraway seeds and stir them in.

Dump the vegetables into the container you plan on using for fermenting. Now's the time to add the starter culture if you're going to use it.

Place a weight in the container and press the sauerkraut down toward the bottom of the container. Press it hard enough to remove any air pockets. The weight should be pressed below the surface of the brine. If not, add a few tablespoons of filtered water at a time until it's covered. There should be enough water to completely cover the top of the weight.

Place the lid on the container and let the sauerkraut ferment for 1 to 2 weeks. Check it regularly and move it to the fridge once it's properly fermented.

Beet Kvass

Beet kvass is a tradition Russian beverage that manages to be both salty and tangy at the same time. Beets are packed with vitamins, minerals and antioxidants, so it's no surprise this drink is considered a probiotic powerhouse. It also looks amazing, since the beets impart their bright red color to the liquid.

Ingredients:

2 beets

3 cups fresh beet juice

Starter culture

1 tablespoon unrefined sea salt

Directions:

Wash the beets and peel them. Cut them into 1" cubes. Place the beets in the fermenting container. Add the beet juice to the container. Fill it to within a few inches of the top of the jar.

Add the starter culture and sea salt. ¼ cup of whey works well as a starter culture for this recipe. Place a weight in the container and press it down on top of the beets. Place a piece of cheesecloth over the top of the container and let it sit at room temperature for a couple days. The kvass is done when it starts to bubble. You should see little white bubbles on top of the liquid within a couple days.

Once the kvass starts bubbling, move it to the fridge. You can remove the beets and reuse them to make another batch of kvass if you'd like. The second batch won't be as strong as the first, but it'll still be pretty good.

Sliced Jalapenos

Have you ever wondered how to make those sliced jalapeno rings you see on nachos? This recipe allows you to take fresh jalapenos and ferment them, creating tasty jalapeno slices that can be added to a number of dishes. Be forewarned; these jalapenos can have quite a kick, especially if you leave in the seeds.

Ingredients:

10 to 15 fresh jalapeno peppers

1 garlic clove, chopped

Starter culture (optional)

2 teaspoons unrefined sea salt

Filtered water

Directions:

Clean the jalapeno peppers and slice them into rings. If you want hotter peppers, leave the seeds in. For milder peppers, remove the seeds from the rings.

Place the jalapenos, sea salt and garlic in the fermenting container. Add filtered water until the water is a couple inches below the top of the container. If you're using starter culture, now's the time to add it.

Place a weight in the container and press it down until the weight is below the surface of the brine. Put the lid on the container and let the container sit for 1 to 2 weeks at room temperature. The jalapenos will change to a duller color and bubbles will form in the brine when they're done.

Move the jalapenos to the fridge when they've fermented to your liking.

Jalapeno Sauerkraut

This sauerkraut adds jalapenos for a spicy kick you don't get from most sauerkraut recipes. My husband loves spicy foods and he complained this recipe wasn't spicy enough. I made a batch that had a couple habanero peppers in it that he loves, but the rest of the family won't touch.

Ingredients:

1 head of cabbage

3 jalapeno peppers

1 carrot

2 cloves garlic

Starter culture (optional)

2 tablespoons unrefined sea salt

Filtered water

Directions:

Wash the vegetables. Shred the cabbage and place it in a large glass bowl. Sprinkle the sea salt on the cabbage. Peel and shred the carrot and add it to the bowl. Mince the garlic cloves and add them to the bowl as well. Cut the peppers into thin slices. It's a good idea to wear gloves while handling the peppers to avoid coming in contact with the juice.

Transfer the contents of the glass bowl to the fermenting container. Add the starter culture now if you plan on using it. The cabbage should have plenty of probiotic bacteria, so the starter culture isn't usually necessary.

Place a weight in the container and press it down. Use the weight to pack the contents of the container down and to remove any air pockets in the sauerkraut. Put the lid on the container and let it sit overnight at room temperature to give the salt time to remove moisture from the vegetables. The next day, push the weight down until it's just below the surface of the brine. If there isn't enough brine, add filtered water to the container until there is.

Place the lid on the container and let the sauerkraut sit at room temperature for a week or two. Taste-test it every couple of days and move it to the fridge when it has fermented to your liking.

Fermented Kohlrabi

For those not familiar with kohlrabi, it's a perennial vegetable that's in the cabbage family. The swollen stem is the part of the kohlrabi that's normally consumed. The leaves are edible as well, but they aren't used in this recipe. Younger, smaller stems are preferable to larger stems, because the bigger stems tend to tough and woody.

Kohlrabi is high in B vitamins and vitamin C. It's also packed full of smaller amounts of other vitamins and minerals, including vitamin E, calcium, iron and potassium. Add in the beneficial bacteria from the fermenting process and you have a tasty dish that's easy to digest and low in calories.

Ingredients:

2 kohlrabi bulbs

1 clove garlic

2 teaspoons dill seeds

Starter culture (optional)

2 teaspoons pickling salt

2 cups filtered water

Directions:

Wash and peel the kohlrabi bulbs. Cut them into large chunks. Mince the garlic. Place the garlic and kohlrabi bulb chunks into the pickling container you plan on using. Add the dill seeds and pickling salt to the container. If you're using starter culture, add it now, following the instructions on the package.

Fill the container with filtered water, leaving a couple inches at the top. Place a weight in the container and press it into the container to ensure the kohlrabi stays submerged below the surface of the brine. If the weight isn't submerged, add water until it is.

Place the lid on the container and let it sit at room temperature for up to a week. Once the kohlrabi has fermented to your liking, move it to the refrigerator.

Kohlrabi Carrot Sauerkraut

The previous recipe just used kohlrabi. This one takes kohlrabi to a whole new level, adding it to sauerkraut. I was a little leery when I first tried this combination, now I rarely make sauerkraut without adding at least a little kohlrabi to the mix.

Ingredients:

1 cup filtered water

1 head of cabbage

2 medium kohlrabi

3 carrots

2 cloves garlic

2 teaspoons starter culture (optional)

2 teaspoons unrefined sea salt

Directions:

Wash and peel the kohlrabi bulbs. Cut them into small chunks. Wash the cabbage and process it in a food processor or cut it into small pieces. Peel and grate the carrots. Mince the garlic.

Mix the vegetables in a bowl. Add the sea salt and gently mash the vegetables with your hands to draw as much water as possible out of the vegetables. Add the starter culture now, if you're planning on using it.

Place the vegetables in the fermenting container(s). Place a weight in each container and press the weight down to compress the sauerkraut and get rid of any air pockets. Place the lid on the container and let it sit overnight. The salt will continue to draw water from the vegetables as it sits. Remove the lid the next day and try to press the weight down further. If the weight can be pressed down to where it's beneath the surface of the brine, you don't have to add any water. If it can't be pressed below the surface, add enough water to get it below the surface.

Put the lid back on the container and let it sit at room temperature for up to a week. Check it after a week. Move it to the fridge if it's fermented to your liking. If not, put the lid back on the container and let it ferment until it's done to your liking.

Dilly Carrots

Carrots are one of my favorite vegetables to lacto-ferment. Dilly carrots are a traditional fermented vegetable that has been around for years. I remember my grandmother eating them when I was a kid. I don't know if she properly fermented them, but I do remember her getting them out of a jar that smelled like pickles.

Ingredients:

5 carrots

2 sprigs fresh dill

2 garlic cloves

Starter culture (optional)

1 tablespoon unrefined sea salt

3 cups filtered water

Directions:

Wash the vegetables. Peel the carrots and cut them into sticks. Chop the dill into fine pieces. Chop the garlic into large chunks. Add all of the vegetables and the dill to the fermenting container.

Combine 1 tablespoon of unrefined sea salt with 3 cups of filtered water to make brine. Pour the brine over the carrots until it's over the top of the carrots. Weight the carrots down by placing a weight on top that fits tightly in the jar. Top off the brine, so there's less than an inch of airspace at the top of the container.

Cover the container and store it at room temperature for 5 to 7 days. Check them and see if they've fermented enough. Once they've fermented properly, move the carrots to the fridge.

Cumin Carrots

Cumin carrots are like dilly carrots, but cumin is added for flavoring instead of the dill. I like to eat the dill carrots on their own. These cumin carrots are better when sliced and served on a salad. They can be cooked, but cooking them will kill most of the probiotic cultures.

Ingredients:

6 to 8 carrots

1 clove garlic

2 tablespoons cumin seeds

Starter culture (optional)

1 tablespoon unrefined sea salt

Filtered water

Directions:

Wash the carrots and garlic. Slice the carrots or cut them into coins. Mince the garlic. Add the carrots, garlic and cumin seeds to the fermenting container.

Mix the sea salt into 3 cups of filtered water. Fill the container with brine until it's over the top of the carrots. Add starter culture now, if you want to use it. Place a weight in the container and press it down until the brine covers the weight. Leave an inch or two of headspace in the container.

Place the lid on the container and let it sit at room temperature for 3 to 4 days. Once the carrots have fermented, move them to the fridge and store them in an airtight container.

Real Fermented Dill Pickles

Most of the pickles sold in the supermarket aren't pickled using traditional fermentation. Instead, they're pickled in vinegar, which leaves them devoid of healthy bacteria and enzymes. If you've never tasted real fermented pickles, you've been missing out. Wait until you bite into one of these. You'll never want to go back to supermarket pickles again.

Ingredients:

10 pickling cucumbers

2 garlic cloves

3 sprigs of dill

2 tablespoons peppercorns

1 tablespoon loose black tea leaf (optional)

Starter culture (optional)

2 tablespoons unrefined sea salt

Filtered water

Directions:

Clean the cucumbers and put them in the fermenting container(s). Peel and mince the garlic and add it to the container. Add the dill, peppercorns and salt. The black tea leaf can be added at this point. The tannins in the tea leaf with help the pickles stay crisp.

Add the water next and then add the starter culture, if you're using it. I prefer to wild ferment my pickles, so I rarely add starter culture. I will occasionally pour some of the left over pickle juice from an old jar into my new jar of pickles to get them off to a good start. This won't work if your old jar is a jar of store-bought pickles that use vinegar in the pickling process.

Pour enough water into the container to cover the top of the pickles. Weight the pickles and make sure there is enough brine to where the weight is completely below the surface.

Put a lid on the container and let the pickles sit for 5 to 7 days. Check them after 5 days and every couple days after that until they've fermented to your liking. When they've fermented enough, move the container to the fridge.

Spicy Pickles

There isn't a lot to say about these pickles, other than they pack a potent punch. If you like spicy stuff, they'll probably suit your palate. On the other hand, if spicy foods aren't your thing, you're better off making one of the other pickle recipes in this book.

Ingredients:

6 to 8 pickling cucumbers

1 clove garlic

½ a sweet onion

1 to 2 tablespoons of chili flakes

1 teaspoon ginger root powder

Starter culture (optional)

2 tablespoons unrefined sea salt

Filtered water

Directions:

Wash the pickling cucumbers and cut them into wedges. They can be left whole if they're small, but they'll take longer to pickle. Mince the garlic and chop the onion up into small pieces. Pack the cucumbers into the fermenting container. Intersperse the onion and garlic between the cucumber wedges.

Mix 2 tablespoons of unrefined sea salt into 4 cups of water and fill the container until the brine is over the top of the cucumbers. Add more brine, if necessary. Add the ginger root powder and chili flakes. If you're planning on using starter culture, now's the time to add it. Place a weight into the container and press it down into the jar to hold the cucumbers down.

Let the container sit at room temperature for a week or two. If you didn't use starter culture, the pickles will take longer to ferment than if you did. Once the pickles have fermented to your liking, move them to the fridge.

Zucchini Pickles

Here's a little known fact—small zucchini make great pickles. OK, maybe it's a well-known fact based on the large number of recipes on the internet, but there isn't a lot of information out there on fermented zucchini pickles. Here's a recipe you can use to ferment zucchini that will leave you with crisp zucchini pickles that taste great and are probiotic.

Ingredients:

4 medium zucchini

4 dill sprigs

1 garlic clove

½ teaspoon coriander seed

1 teaspoon dill seed

Starter culture (optional)

2 tablespoons unrefined sea salt

Filtered water

Directions:

Clean and cut the zucchini into quarters. If the container you're using is too small, keep cutting them in half until the pieces will fit. Place the zucchini pieces into the container(s). Cut the garlic clove up and add it to the container. Add the dill sprigs, coriander seeds and dill seeds.

Sprinkle the unrefined sea salt over the vegetables. Fill the container to within a few inches of the top with filtered water. Add the starter culture now if you plan on using it. Place a weight into the container and press it down over the zucchini. Add water until the weight is below the surface of the brine.

Seal the container and wait 5 to 7 days. After 5 days have passed, check the zucchini pickles to see if they're fermenting. If they're fermented to your liking, move them to the fridge. If not, let them ferment for a longer period of time before moving them.

Cultured Olives

Olives have always held a special place in my heart. As a kid, I remember running around with "olive fingers" trying to gross my younger siblings out. Now, I have a blast watching my kids do the same.

I spent years buying jars of olives from the store. I never gave much thought to curing them myself until the last couple years when I got started with fermenting. While store-bought olives are often treated with lye, you choose what you add to the olives you make at home, making them the healthier choice.

Ingredients:

Olives

5 tablespoons unrefined sea salt

Filtered water

Directions:

Wash the olives. If they're still on the branches, remove the stems and leaves. Throw out any damaged olives.

Each olive needs to be split open. You can do this by scoring each olive all the way around with a sharp knife. Olives that aren't split open can take years to cure. Cracking them speeds the time needed for curing up to a week or two. Uncured olives are all but inedible because of how bitter they are. The curing process removes some of the bitterness. The longer the olives are cured, the less bitter they'll be.

Place the olives in the container. Mix the sea salt with enough water to completely submerge the olives and stir the salt into the water. Pour the brine into the container. Weight the olives to make sure they stay submerged. Place the lid on the container and let the olives sit at room temperature for one to two weeks. Change the brine every couple of days.

Check the olives periodically to see if they're properly curing. Fresh olives are a bright green color. As they cure, they change to the olive color we're all used to. If the olives look good, take one out and taste it. Olives that aren't done curing will be extremely bitter.

Once the olives are done curing, change the brine one last time. Add garlic, ginger and coriander to the brine. Move the olives to the fridge.

Probiotic Garlic

Garlic is good for you on its own. It's even better for you when it's fermented. This recipe is super easy, so there's no excuse for not having fermented garlic on hand when you want it. This garlic can be used in most recipes that call for regular garlic. I prefer to use it in recipes that don't use heat, because I don't want to kill the probiotic cultures.

Ingredients:

5 to 10 garlic heads

2 teaspoons unrefined sea salt

Starter culture (optional)

Filtered water

Directions:

The first step is the most time-consuming step in the process. Peel all the garlic heads and separate the cloves. Be careful not to damage the cloves while peeling them.

Place the garlic cloves, sea salt and water into the fermenting container. Add the starter culture now, if you want to use it. Fill the container with filtered water until the cloves are covered. Place a weight in the container and press it down to where the weight is below the surface of the water. Garlic is heavy and tends to sink to the bottom of the container, so you could probably get away with not using a weight.

Let the garlic ferment at room temperature for 5 to 7 days. You may find your garlic cloves take on a blue or green tint as they ferment. As long as there are no other signs of spoilage, this is a normal reaction between the garlic and chemical compounds in the water.

Once the garlic has fermented to your liking, move it to the refrigerator or another cool location to store it until you're ready to eat it.

Fermented Asparagus

Here's a forgiving recipe perfect for the beginning fermenter. All you have to do is add asparagus to the fermenting container, add a couple ingredients and seal it up. A week later you've got delicious fermented asparagus.

Ingredients:

10 to 20 asparagus stalks

1 organic lemon

½ onion

1 garlic clove

Starter culture (optional)

2 teaspoons unrefined sea salt

Filtered water

Directions:

Wash the vegetables. Cut the tough part at the bottom of each asparagus stalk off and discard it. Place the asparagus stalks into the fermenting container. Cut the lemon in half and squeeze the juice into the container. Chop the onion and disperse it between the asparagus spears. Mince the garlic and do the same.

Add the sea salt to enough filtered water to create a brine you can use to fill the fermenting container full enough to cover the asparagus. Stir the starter culture in if you plan on using it. Pour the brine over the asparagus. Make sure the asparagus is completely covered with brine.

Weight the asparagus down by placing something on top of it that's heavy enough to hold it beneath the surface of the brine. Place the lid on the container and let it sit for a week. Check the asparagus and move it to the fridge once it's fermenting nicely.

Fermented Broccoli and Cauliflower

This recipe uses cruciferous vegetables, namely cauliflower, cabbage and broccoli. Feel free to add any other cruciferous veggies you'd like. Kohlrabi and kale are both good additions. For an interesting look, try mixing cabbage types and using different colors of cabbage.

Ingredients:

1 cup broccoli florets

1 cup cauliflower florets

¼ head of cabbage

½ onion

½ teaspoon oregano

1 teaspoon thyme

1 teaspoon basil

Starter culture (optional)

3 teaspoons unrefined sea salt

Filtered water

Directions:

Wash the vegetables. Shred the cabbage and place it in the fermenting container. Sprinkle the sea salt over the cabbage. If the broccoli and cauliflower florets are small, they can be left as-is. If they're too big, cut or break them into smaller pieces. Slice the onion into thin slices. Add all the vegetables to the container.

Add water until it's over the top of the vegetables. Add the seasonings and the sea salt to a few cups of water and stir it in. If you're using starter culture, add it now. It isn't a necessity because the cabbage should have a lot of healthy bacteria on it. Place a weight over the top of the vegetables and push it down until the weight is below the surface of the brine.

Put the lid on the container and store it at room temperature for 5 to 7 days. Move it to the refrigerator once it's fermented.

Fermented Celery

Regular celery has always tasted bland to me. This recipe ferments it and gives it a tangy, sour flavor that's much more appealing.

Ingredients:

1 to 2 bunches of celery

½ onion

3 garlic cloves

1 dill sprig

1 tablespoon unrefined sea salt

Starter culture (optional)

Filtered water

Directions:

Wash the vegetables. Cut the celery into pieces that'll fit into your container leaving a few inches of headspace. Chop the onion into small pieces and mince the garlic. Place the celery into the container. Disperse the onion, garlic and dill between the celery.

Mix the salt with enough filtered water to completely cover the celery. Weight the celery in order to keep it below the surface of the brine. Close the container and let it sit for 1 to 2 weeks at room temperature.

Check the celery every couple of days and move it to the fridge once it has fermented to your liking.

Fermented Green Beans

I grow green beans in my garden and come harvest time always used to have way more green beans than I could handle. That is, until I started fermented them. Now I can enjoy the green beans from my garden year-round. I get fresh green beans when I harvest them and can enjoy pickled green beans the rest of the year.

I've noticed that most recipes for fermented green beans call for blanching the green beans before fermenting them. The blanching process kills off any good bacteria living on the green beans. If you decide to follow one of those recipes and blanch your green beans, you have to use whey or some other form of starter culture to add the beneficial bacteria back to the green beans. This process seems counterintuitive to me, but it does make the green beans more uniform in appearance and texture as they ferment.

There is some misinformation out there stating green beans are toxic if they aren't blanched. Green beans are high in lectins and can cause trouble in sensitive individuals when consumed in large amounts raw. Lectins cause intestinal damage and may cause leaky gut syndrome, which is a hole in the intestines that leaks toxins and partially digested foods into the body. When lectins escape, they bind to all different kinds of tissue in the body, causing the body to react negatively.

Studies have shown natural fermentation to effectively reduce lectin in food. Since the fermentation process naturally reduces lectin, blanching likely isn't a necessity from a safety standpoint. Whether it's a necessity to ensure a uniform texture is a completely different story. It's largely up to you whether you blanch your green beans, but if you do, make sure you add bacterial culture back to the fermentation. Otherwise, you may end up with pickled green beans that are devoid of the beneficial flora found in fermented beans.

Ingredients:

1 to 2 cups fresh green beans

1 small carrot

1 clove garlic

Starter culture (optional, as long as green beans aren't blanched)

2 teaspoons unrefined sea salt

Filtered water

Directions:

Wash the vegetables. Cut the ends off of the green beans and shred the carrot. Chop the garlic into small pieces. Pack the green beans into the fermenting container. As you pack the green beans in, add the shredded carrot and garlic, so it's distributed throughout the beans.

Add water and salt to the container. The brine should be above the top of the green beans. Place a weight in the container. Press it down until it's below the surface of the brine. This step may not seem necessary because the green beans are packed in tightly, but they'll shrink as they ferment and may float to the top. The weight will ensure the green beans stay below the surface of the brine.

Place the lid on the container and let the green beans ferment for 5 to 7 days. Check the flavor when you notice the bubbling has slowed down a bit. Once they're to your liking, move them to the fridge.

Fermented Mushrooms

If I had to pick a favorite vegetable, mushrooms would be at the top of the list. I love them sautéed, fried and raw on salads. For some reason, it never occurred to me to ferment them until recently. Now that I've tried it, I'm hooked. These mushrooms are good on their own and they go great with spaghetti sauce.

Ingredients:

2 cups mushrooms

1 garlic clove

½ onion

1 tablespoon marjoram

1 tablespoon thyme

1 tablespoon oregano

Starter culture (optional, as long as the mushrooms aren't blanched)

2 teaspoons unrefined sea salt

Filtered water

Directions:

Wash the mushrooms and slice them. Mince the garlic clove. Wash the onion and dice it. Add the mushrooms, garlic and diced onion to the fermenting container.

Combine 3 cups of filtered water with the sea salt and stir the salt in. Add the starter culture at this time, if you're planning on using it. Pour the brine over the mushrooms until they're covered. Place a weight in the container to hold the mushrooms below the surface of the brine. Add more brine, if necessary.

Place the lid on the container and store the container at room temperature. Leave it for 5 to 7 days. Once the mushrooms have fermented to your liking, move them to the fridge.

Traditional Kimchi

The first time I tried kimchi I was around 15 years old. I was at a Korean friend's house and her parents were eating it. They offered me some and I graciously accepted, only to find it tasted like nothing I'd ever experienced. At the time, I'd never heard of fermented foods, let alone tried them, so it was a new experience that wasn't exactly pleasant.

Fast forward a few years—OK, a lot of years—and I've got a newfound appreciation for kimchi. It's a traditional Korean dish that is a healthy staple in the Korean diet. It's somewhat of an acquired taste, but if you like cultured foods, it isn't too tough to get used to. One warning—this recipe is a bit spicy. If you don't like spicy food, eliminate the red pepper powder.

Ingredients:

1 head Chinese cabbage

½ cup green onions, chopped

3 cloves garlic

1 tablespoon ginger root, minced

3 tablespoons Korean red pepper powder

2 teaspoons unrefined sea salt

Filtered water

Directions:

Wash the vegetables. Chop the cabbage into large chunks. Chop the green onions. Mince the cloves of garlic. Peel the ginger root and mince it. Add the red pepper powder and sea salt to the vegetables and mix them together in a large bowl.

Mash the vegetables to get as much water as you can out of them. Place the vegetables in the fermenting container. Place a weight in the container and mash the vegetables down. Push the weight down until it's beneath the surface of the brine. If there isn't enough brine, add filtered water until there is.

Place the lid on the container and seal it tightly. Leave the container at room temperature for a week or two. Check it after a week to see if it's fermenting. If it's good, move it to the refrigerator. If not, let it sit at room temperature until it's ready before moving it to the fridge.

Natto

Natto is a traditional Japanese dish made of fermented soybeans. It's sticky, smells bad and doesn't taste much better than it smells. It's normally served at breakfast time in Japan because it's thought to increase strength and prepare those brave enough to eat it for the day ahead.

Natto is definitely an acquired taste, but it really is good for you. It's packed full of vitamins and healthy probiotic cultures and is thought by some to be the reason Japanese people live long lives in spite of bad habits like smoking and drinking. Whether this is true or not is up for debate, but one thing's for certain. If you can eat it, natto probably isn't going to hurt you.

Make sure you source organic non-GMO soybeans when you make natto. More than 90% of the soy crops grown in the United States are genetically modified, so this could prove a bit difficult. Check your local health foods stores. If that fails, you can always find them online. Just be sure to get them from a reputable source.

Ingredients:

4 cups organic dried soybeans

1 spoonful Natto spores

12 cups filtered water

Directions:

Wash the soybeans and place them in a large glass bowl. Pour the 12 cups of filtered water into the bowl with the beans and let them soak for at least 12 hours. The beans will swell to more than twice the size they were dry.

The next step is to boil the soybeans or steam them in a pressure cooker until they're soft enough for fermentation. If you're boiling them, add a tablespoon of salt to 5 cups filtered water and boil the beans for at least 6 hours, or until the beans are soft. If you're steaming them in a pressure cooker, the cook time is reduced to less than an hour. Make sure the pot or cooker you use is made from a non-reactive material like stainless steel.

Transfer the beans into another sterile nonreactive pot. It's time to add the natto spores. This is the natto starter culture. Starter culture is optional for most of the recipes in this book, but it has to be added to the natto because the soybeans have been cooked for a long time and all beneficial bacteria will have died off. Follow the instructions that came with the natto spores and add them to pot. Mix the natto spores into the soybeans while the beans are still hot. Be careful not to smash the beans while mixing in the spores.

Add a cup of natto beans to each container. Place cheesecloth over the container and place the lid on tightly. Natto needs to be kept warm while it ferments. The temperature needs to be kept near 100 degrees F for the first 24 hours. This can be done in a special natto warmer, an oven, a dehydrator or even an ice chest into which you place jars of hot water along with the containers of natto.

After the natto has fermented for 24 hours, remove it from the heat and let it cool to room temperature. Take the lid off and remove the cheesecloth. Put the lid back on and refrigerate the natto.

This stuff is going to smell pretty strong when you remove the lid. It should be smelly and sticky. If not, let it age for a while longer before eating it.

Escabeche

Escabeche is a traditional Mexican dish usually served as a side dish. It has jalapenos, sweet peppers, onions and garlic in it, and there are a number of variations that add all sorts of other vegetables to the mix. It goes well with street tacos and other Mexican foods. It also makes a great snack if you're looking for something fermented to munch on.

Jalapeno peppers are fairly hot and handling them can get juice on your hands and fingers that can burn sensitive tissue. Wearing gloves while handling the peppers can save you from a lot of discomfort later when you accidentally rub your eyes or go to the bathroom and brush your hand against a sensitive area.

Ingredients:

15 large jalapeno peppers

1 red bell pepper

1 green bell pepper

3 medium carrots

1 medium onion

4 cloves garlic

2 tablespoons peppercorns

1 tablespoon dried oregano

Starter culture (optional)

3 teaspoons unrefined sea salt

Filtered water

Directions:

Wash the vegetables. Slice the jalapenos into rings. Remove the seeds from the bell peppers and slice them into chunks. Peel the carrots and slice them into coins. Chop the onion into small pieces. Mince the garlic cloves. Place the vegetables in a large glass bowl.

Stir the peppercorns, dried oregano and sea salt into 2 cups of water. If you're using starter culture, add it now and stir it in. Fill the container(s) with the vegetables and any liquid in the bowl. Place a weight in each container and press it down until the brine is over the top of the weight. If there isn't enough brine, add filtered water until the brine is over the top of the weight.

Place the lid on the container and store it at room temperature for 3 to 5 days. Move the vegetables to the fridge once they start fermenting.

Cultured Salsa

I love fresh salsa. It's one of my favorite condiments, and I use it on everything from eggs to burritos. I never thought I'd replace fresh salsa in my diet, and I didn't think I would ever feel the urge because it's good for you. Then I discovered fermenting and found that fermented salsa tastes every bit as good, if not better, than fresh salsa.

This recipe is good on its own. If you want it to be less spicy, cut back on the jalapeno peppers. If you're like my husband and love spicy foods, try adding a single diced habanero pepper to the recipe. Add a second habanero if you're feeling particularly sadistic.

Ingredients:

7 to 10 tomatoes

3 jalapeno peppers

1 medium onion

1 clove garlic

3 tablespoons lemon juice

1 teaspoon dried cumin

1 teaspoon oregano

Cayenne pepper, to taste

Cilantro, to taste

Starter culture (optional)

3 teaspoons unrefined sea salt

Filtered water

Directions:

Wash the vegetables. Mince the vegetables individually. Remove the seeds from the peppers before mincing them. This can be done by hand or using a food processor. Don't mince all of the vegetables at once unless you want salsa the consistency of paste.

Add the seasonings to the salsa. If you're using starter culture, now's the time to add it. Stir the salt in and place the salsa in the fermenting container. Place a weight in the container and press it down to get rid of any air pockets. Add filtered water, as needed. The salsa shouldn't need much water added, as the tomatoes should have plenty of moisture.

Place the lid on the container and let it ferment at room temperature for 3 to 5 days before moving it to the fridge.

Fermented Ketchup

Ketchup is without a doubt the most used condiment in America. We put it on everything. French fries, meat, eggs . . . you name it, there's probably someone putting ketchup on it.

The problem with the ketchup you buy in stores is, even though it's made from tomatoes, it really isn't good for you. For one, the tomatoes are often cooked at high heat and high pressure, destroying much of the health value. Then high fructose corn syrup is added to sweeten the ketchup. High fructose corn syrup is basically sugar, which isn't good, and it's more than likely made from genetically modified corn, which is even worse. In addition to high fructose corn syrup, many ketchup brands also contain regular corn syrup, which again is probably made from GMO-corn.

So what's a ketchup lover to do? You can use this recipe to create fermented ketchup that's completely natural and uses non-GMO tomatoes. It's fermented, too, which means it'll give any food you put it on a healthy probiotic boost.

This recipe calls for organic tomato paste. You can make your own, but unless you want to spend countless hours in the kitchen reducing the tomatoes to paste, you're probably better off just buying it.

Ingredients:

2 cups organic tomato paste

2 cloves garlic

½ cup fish sauce

¼ cup organic maple syrup

Pepper, to taste

Starter culture

1 ½ tablespoons unrefined sea salt

Directions:

Mince the clove of garlic. Combine the garlic, tomato paste, fish sauce, maple syrup and sea salt in a glass bowl and pour the mixture into the fermenting container. Leave an inch or two of headspace at the top of the jar. Add pepper, to taste.

Stir in the starter culture. You can use whey or vegetable starter culture. It's necessary in this recipe because you don't know whether the tomato paste has beneficial bacteria in it. It's unlikely they've survived the processing the paste went through before it was packaged.

Place the lid on the container and let the ketchup ferment for 3 to 5 days at room temperature. The ketchup doesn't usually get fizzy, so don't worry if bubbles don't form. Move the ketchup to the refrigerator, where it should keep for 6 to 8 months.

Homemade Root Beer

OK, this recipe technically doesn't use any vegetables, but it does use spices and roots. It's also absolutely delicious and much better for you than the root beer sold in stores, which has zero health value. This root beer, on the other hand, is fermented, so you're adding healthy probiotic bacteria to your digestive system when you drink it. It does have sugar, but it's cane sugar instead of the high fructose corn syrup found in commercial root beer.

This fermented root beer recipe adds mild carbonation through lacto-fermentation. It won't be as strongly carbonated as the soda you're used to. Instead, there will be a slight fizz to it. If you want more fizz, mineral water can be added when you're ready to drink it.

Ingredients:

¼ cup dried sarsaparilla root

¼ cup sassafras root

1 cup unrefined cane sugar

2 teaspoons licorice root

1 teaspoon juniper berries

1 teaspoon ground cinnamon stick

Starter culture

8 cups filtered water

Directions:

Place the water in pot and bring it to a rolling boil. Add the sarsaparilla root, sassafras root, cane sugar, licorice root, juniper berries and cinnamon and let it simmer for 25 minutes. Remove the root beer from the heat and let it sit for another 20 minutes. The root beer should be allowed to cool to room temperature.

Strain the liquid through fine mesh or cheesecloth to remove the solids from the liquid. Place the strained root beer into the bottle(s). Add ¼ cup of whey (or some other starter culture) to the liquid. Cap the bottle tightly and let the root beer sit at room temperature for 3 to 5 days. Once the carbonation bubbles start to appear, move the root beer to the fridge.

Don't Throw the Brine Out

Don't dump the brine down the sink once you've finished the food you've fermented. The brine is packed full of probiotic goodness and is almost as good for you as the fermented vegetables.

There are a handful of uses for the brine, including the following:

- **Drink it.** If you can get past the salty flavor, drinking the brine is the most direct route to consuming it. The probiotic brine will be strong in flavor, so you may have to add water to it to make it palatable.
- **Use it to jumpstart another ferment.** A few tablespoons of brine from an old ferment can be added to a new ferment to get it off to a good start.
- **Add it to a smoothie.** Don't like the thought of drinking brine? No worries; it can be added to a smoothie to give it a probiotic boost. You can enjoy all the health benefits of the brine without having to choke it down.
- **Drizzle it over food.** Brine can be drizzled over a number of food items, including meats and salads.

FAQ

There are a number of questions that may arise while fermenting. This section seeks to cover as many of them as possible.

What Temperature Range Is Acceptable For Fermenting?

The ideal temperature range to ferment at is 70 to 75 degrees F for most vegetables. This allows for maximum growth of beneficial bacteria. If fermenting at these temperatures isn't possible, fermenting can be done at hotter and cooler temperatures, but it'll require watching the fermenting vegetables closely.

Foods that are fermented at temperatures outside the ideal range will have to be monitored for problems that may arise. Foods are more likely to go bad when fermented at temperatures that aren't ideal. When fermenting at higher temperatures than those that are ideal, watch vegetables closely because they tend to go soft quickly. Cooler temperatures will slow the fermenting process to a crawl.

Should Fermenting Be Done In the Dark or the Light?

The fermenting container needs to be kept out of direct light, especially if the container is made of clear glass. Sunlight is particularly harmful, as it can break down the lactic acid and can heat the contents of the container beyond the optimal temperature. If you're planning on fermenting in an area that gets a lot of direct light, wrap the fermenting vessel(s) in a towel or sheet.

What Should Be Done If Mold Starts to Form?

Mold can form on vegetables for a number of reasons. Unsanitary containers and dirty vegetables can introduce harmful microorganisms to the fermenting process. Too warm or cold of conditions or too much oxygen being allowed into the container can also cause mold. Leaving air pockets in the food can leave you with moldy spots where the air pockets are. Sometimes, it seems like you do everything right and mold still forms.

There are a number of sources that indicate it's safe to remove the moldy food from the top of the container and eat the food beneath it. The problem with this recommendation is there's no way to tell if the rest of the food has been contaminated. When mold spreads, it sends out tendrils that are invisible to the naked eye, so food that doesn't show visible signs of infection could still be infected.

For this reason, it's best to throw moldy foods out and start fresh.

One more note . . . Vegetables that turn pink that aren't supposed to turn pink are indicative of unhealthy organisms growing in the container. These vegetables need to be discarded as well.

Why Is There a Lot of Foam?

Foam is a natural part of the fermentation process. The foam forms as the gases created by the chemical reaction float to the surface of the brine. Foam is usually indicative of a healthy fermentation process, but it isn't always present when vegetables are fermenting.

Some ferments can bubble so much the foam bubbles out of the container. This leads some people to believe the food inside has gone bad. While this can make quite a mess, it's a normal part of the fermentation process. This is the reason containers that are completely airtight need to be opened every couple of days to release the pressure. The problem with doing this is it adds oxygen to the container. A better option is to use airlock containers designed to release gases as pressure builds.

Why Are the Vegetables Slimy?

Slimy vegetables are an indication that something went wrong during the fermentation process. The slime is a byproduct of the presence of organisms you shouldn't consume. This can occur when too little salt is used or too much oxygen is allowed into the fermenting container. If vegetables are slimy, discard them and try again. The same thing goes for slimy brine. If the brine becomes viscous, toss it out.

Why Is There White Stuff Floating Near the Top of the Container?

A layer of yeast can form near the top of the container. The brine will turn a cloudy white color and the yeast will pool at the top. Most people's first assumption is this is mold starting to form and the food inside the container is going bad.

Most of the time, a white layer near the surface of the brine isn't mold. It's actually a type of yeast that forms as part of the fermentation process. It doesn't always form, but will appear when conditions are right. It is common when containers that aren't airtight are used and when the vegetables in a container aren't kept below the surface of the brine. It's less common when a weighting system is used to keep the vegetables below the brine.

This white yeast can be removed and the vegetables should be fine. It's important to be sure you're removing yeast and not mold. Mold can be white, but it usually appears as a fuzzy growth and can have other colors interspersed throughout the mold.

What Should Properly Fermented Food Smell Like?

Fermented food is supposed to smell sour, and the smell can be fairly strong, especially when the jar is first opened after being allowed to ferment for a long period of time. The first few times through the fermenting process, you may find yourself questioning whether or not the food has gone bad.

Food that has turned will have a rotten stench to it. Sour is good. Rotten isn't. It's best to err on the side of caution. If a batch of fermented vegetables doesn't smell right, discard it and try again.

Do the Vegetables Need to Be Peeled Before Fermenting?

That depends. If you're using organic vegetables, the skin can usually be left on during the fermentation process.

It's actually beneficial to leave the skin on because the skin of the vegetable is the part that contains the most beneficial organisms.

If you're using regular produce that isn't organic, the peel can harbor large amounts of pesticides. You're better off peeling the vegetables and discarding the peel. When you peel the vegetables, starter culture should be used because most of the beneficial bacteria will be removed with the peel.

Why Did the Vegetables Go Soft?

There are a lot of factors that can cause vegetables to go soft. Too much heat is the most common reason because it speeds up the fermentation process. Try adding a grape leaf or a tea leaf to the brine to add tannin to it.

Vegetables that are allowed to ferment for long periods of time will start to soften. This is part of the natural fermenting process. It's normal, but vegetables that are allowed to go too soft are difficult to eat because of the consistency and strong sour taste and smell. Most fermenters throw vegetables that get too soft away and make another batch.

Contact the Author

I sincerely hope you enjoyed this book and are able to make use of the tips, techniques and recipes contained herein. I'd love to hear from you. If you have additional tips, techniques or recipes you'd like to see in future iterations of the book, send me an e-mail at the following address:

mike_rashelle@yahoo.com

I'll get back to you as soon as possible.

Other Books You May Be Interested In

Essential oils are the concentrated essence of plants. Learn all about their many therapeutic qualities in the following book.

The Aromatherapy & Essential Oils Handbook

http://www.amazon.com/dp/B00BECCJXY

Diet plays a huge role in healthy living. If you're interested in healthy eating, there are a number of healthy foods you may be interested in adding to your diet. The following books may be of interest to you.

The Coconut Flour Cookbook: Delicious Gluten Free Coconut Flour Recipes

http://www.amazon.com/dp/B00CC0JFPM

The Almond Flour Cookbook: 30 Delicious and Gluten Free Recipes

The Quinoa Cookbook: Healthy and Delicious Quinoa Recipes (Superfood Cookbooks)

http://www.amazon.com/dp/B00B2T2420

The Coconut Oil Guide: How to Stay Healthy, Lose Weight and Feel Good through Use of Coconut Oil

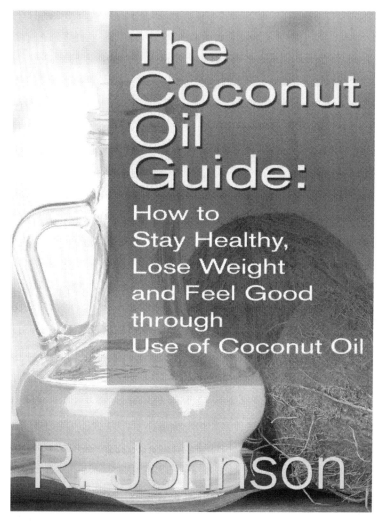

http://www.amazon.com/The-Coconut-Oil-Guide-ebook/dp/B00CESE3HC/

21206570R00072

Printed in Great Britain
by Amazon